P9-DOG-590

J. Michael and Cindy...
cannot even begin to relate to
your loss - but know you are loved
by and supported by anyone that's ever
been touched by you - he will be forever
young and always in your heart...

Much love,
Jim and Cheryl

Katie Mom
I loved him dearly.
And I will miss him
greatly. But there is
nothing harder than
loosing a child. I hope
this book helps you as
it helped me! I read
it a lot in the first
few months. He's with
his kids now. They will
take care of him
I love you so!
your daughter
Cindy P?

J. Michael &
Cindy ~ There
are no words, so
we just want to
send hugs, love,
& our prayers &
with much love,
Mark & Suzi

Grieve Not

COMPILED BY

BLUE LANTERN STUDIO

LAUGHING ELEPHANT   MMI

FOR THE FAMILY
& FRIENDS OF

YOM TOBY HOGAN

AD ASTRA PER ASPERA

MAY 17, 1976 - FEBRUARY 20, 2001

COPYRIGHT © 2001 BLUE LANTERN STUDIO

ISBN 1-883211-43-3

FIRST PRINTING ALL RIGHTS RESERVED
PRINTED IN SINGAPORE

LAUGHING ELEPHANT BOOKS
POST OFFICE BOX 31969 SEATTLE WASHINGTON 98103

*Do not stand
at my grave and weep.*

I am not there,
I do not sleep.

I am the thousand
winds that blow.

I am diamond

glints on snow.

I am the sunlight
on ripened grain.

I am gentle autumnal rain.

When you waken

in the morning hush,

I am the soft

uplifting rush

Of quiet birds

in circled flight.

I am the soft stars
that shine at night.

Do not stand at
my grave and cry

I am not there.
I did not die.

PICTURE CREDITS

PICTURE CREDITS

COLOPHON

DESIGNED AT BLUE LANTERN STUDIO
BY SACHEVERELL DARLING
AND MIKE HARRISON

TYPESET IN PALACE SCRIPT & CENTAUR